THIS WAY
TO HAPPINESS

*To help you
appreciate anew
the beauty and wonder
of living*

✿ ✿ ————————————————

by
Gilbert Hay, M.S.SS.T.

✿ ✿ — *SIMON AND SCHUSTER New York*

LIBRARY OF CONGRESS CATALOG CARD NUMBER: 67-13028
DESIGNED BY EDITH FOWLER
MANUFACTURED IN THE UNITED STATES OF AMERICA
BY VAIL-BALLOU PRESS, INC., BINGHAMTON, NEW YORK

For arrangements made with various authors and publishing houses where copyrighted material was permitted to be reprinted and for the courtesy extended by them, the following acknowledgments are gratefully made. All possible care has been taken to trace the ownership of every selection included and to make full acknowledgment for its use. If any errors have accidentally occurred, they will be corrected in subsequent editions, provided notification is sent to the publisher.

The Bobbs-Merrill Company, Inc., for permission to use "In Tune with the Infinite" from The Best of Ralph Waldo Trine, *copyright © 1957 by The Bobbs-Merrill Company, Inc.; and for "The Measure of Man" from* The Measure of Man, *copyright © 1953, 1954 by Joseph Wood Krutch.*

Doubleday & Company, Inc., for permission to use material from How to Live on 24 Hours a Day *by Arnold Bennett, copyright 1910 by Doubleday & Company, Inc.*

Devin-Adair Company for permission to use material by Austin O'Malley.

E. P. Dutton & Co., Inc., for permission to use material from Marriage *by William Lyon Phelps; and for material from* The Ultimate Belief *by A. Clutton-Brock.*

The Estate of Albert Einstein for permission to use material by Albert Einstein.

Harper & Row, Inc., for permission to use material by Harry Emerson Fosdick.

Hartmore House for permission to use material from A Treasury of the Art of Living *edited by Sidney Greenberg, copyright © 1963 by Hartmore House.*

Contents

*There are single thoughts
that contain the essence of a whole volume,
single sentences that have the beauties
of a large work.*
                    —JOSEPH JOUBERT

❁   ❁

*I pick up my favorite quotations
and store them in my mind as ready armor,
offensive or defensive,
amid the struggle of this
turbulent existence.*
                    —ROBERT BURNS

❀ ❀ ❀

This
Wonderful
Day

This new day is given to us,
uncluttered, fresh and clean.
Yesterday's troubles are in the past;
tomorrow's may never be seen.
God has granted us this new
day to do with as we will . . .
Let's fill it with kindness and happiness,
love, joy and good will!

❀   ❀

Every day is a gift
from heaven.
Let me enjoy today
that which it bestows on me.
Today belongs
not more to the young
than to the old,
and tomorrow
belongs to no one.
              —MANCROIX

For my own part,
I live every day as if this
were the first day I had ever seen
and the last day I were going to see.

—WILLIAM LYON PHELPS

❁ ❁

You wake up in the morning,
and lo!
your purse is magically filled
with twenty-four hours
of the unmanufactured tissue
of the universe of your life.
It is yours.
It is the most precious of possessions.
No one can take it from you.
It is unstealable.
And no one receives
either more or less
than you receive.

—ARNOLD BENNETT

Be grateful for each new day.
A new day that you
have never lived before.
Twenty-four new, fresh,
unexplored hours
to use usefully and joyfully.
You can squander, neglect
or use them.
Life will be richer or poorer
by the way you use today.

❁ ❁

Start the morning
with this thought:
I've never lived this day before;
this will be a happy day;
it will be a day
of great accomplishment.

Life begins each morning.
Each morning is the open door
to a new world
—new vistas, new aims, new tryings.
                    —LEIGH HODGES

No man ever sank
beneath the burden of the day.
It is when tomorrow's burden
is added to the burden of today
that the weight
is more than we can bear.
It is delightfully easy
to live one day at a time.
                    —GEORGE MACDONALD

Finish every day and be done with it.
You have done what you could.
Some blunders and absurdities
no doubt crept in;
forget them as soon as you can.
Today is a new day;
begin it well and serenely
and with too high a spirit
to be cumbered with your old nonsense.
This day is all that is good and fair.
It is too dear,
with its hopes and invitations,
to waste a moment on yesterdays.

—RALPH WALDO EMERSON

"This is the day which the Lord has made."
We shall never overtake tomorrow.
Wherever we are, it will always be today.
So if ever we are to be glad we are alive,
and relaxed in a childlike gala mood
of appreciation for all things
we have to enjoy,
and of gratitude to their Giver,
now is the time to begin.
"This is the day which the Lord has made;
we will rejoice and be glad in it."
That is common sense.
And, even if we try,
we cannot fret and worry
at the same time we are rejoicing
and being glad.

—RUSSELL HENRY STAFFORD

To me,
every hour of the day and night
is an unspeakable perfect miracle.

—WALT WHITMAN

❁   ❁   ❁

Happiness

We must not look outside
for happiness,
but in ourselves, in our own minds.
The kingdom of God
is within you.

—JOHN LUBBOCK

We act as though
comfort and luxury
were the chief requirements
of life,
when all we need
to make us really happy
is something
to be enthusiastic about.

—CHARLES KINGSLEY

Domestic happiness depends
upon the ability
to overlook.
　　　—ROY L. SMITH

Happiness grows
at our own firesides,
and is not to be picked
in strangers' gardens.
　　　—DOUGLAS JERROLD

He enjoys much
who is thankful for little.
A grateful mind
is both a great and happy mind.
　　　—THOMAS SECKER

Most folks are
about as happy
as they make up their minds to be.
　　　—ABRAHAM LINCOLN

❀　❀

One of the hardest lessons
we have to learn in this life,
and one that many persons never learn,
is to see the divine,
the celestial, the pure
in the common—the near at hand.
To see that heaven lies about us
here in this world.
　　　—JOHN BURROUGHS

❀　❀

Success is getting what you want;
happiness is wanting
what you get.

If you are alive and happy today,
that is enough.
Tomorrow never comes until it is today.
There's no reason
why each succeeding day
should not be as happy,
or happier,
than your yesterdays
if you mentally picture
a continuation of this happiness
in your future.

—HAROLD SHERMAN

We die daily—
happy those
who daily come to life as well.
                —GEORGE MACDONALD

The harvest of happiness
is most often reaped
by the hands of helpfulness.

Happiness is
a thing to be practiced,
like the violin.
                —JOHN LUBBOCK

Happy the man who has broken the chains
which hurt the mind,
and has given up worrying
once and for all.
        —OVID

I don't know
what your destiny will be,
but one thing I know,
the only ones among you
who will be really happy
are those who have sought and found
how to serve.
        —ALBERT SCHWEITZER

To do something, however small,
to make others happier and better,
is the highest ambition,
the most elevating hope,
which can inspire a human being.
—JOHN LUBBOCK

❁　❁

The secret of happiness and prosperity,
in this world
as in the world to come,
lies in thinking of
the welfare of others first,
and not taking one's self
too seriously.
—JAMES H. KINDELBERGER

Everybody really knows what to do
to have his life filled with joy.
What is it?
Quit hating people; start loving them.
Quit being mad at people; start liking them.
Quit doing wrong;
quit being filled with fear.
Quit thinking about yourself
and go out and do something for other people.
Everybody knows what you have to do
to be happy.
But the test lies in the final words:
"If you know these things,
happy are you if you do them."

—NORMAN VINCENT PEALE

One of the most tragic things I know
about human nature
is that all of us tend to put off living.
We dream of some magical rose garden
over the horizon—
instead of enjoying the roses
that are blooming
outside our window today.

—DALE CARNEGIE

Every job has drudgery,
whether it is in the home,
in the professional school
or in the office.
The first secret of happiness
is the recognition of
this fundamental fact.

—M. C. MCINTOSH

A happy life is not built up
of tours abroad or pleasant holidays,
but of little clumps of violets
noticed by the roadside,
hidden away
almost so that only those can see them
who have God's peace and love
in their hearts;
in one long continuous chain
of little joys,
little whispers from the spiritual world,
and little gleams of sunshine
on our daily work.

—EDWARD WILSON

Not what we have,
but what we enjoy
constitutes our abundance.

—J. PETIT-SENN

Let the weakest,
let the humblest remember
that in his daily course he can,
if he will,
shed around him almost a heaven.
Kind words, sympathizing attentions,
watchfulness against
wounding men's sensitiveness—
these cost but little,
but are priceless in their value.
Are they not almost staples
of our daily happiness?
From hour to hour,
from moment to moment,
we are supported, blest,
by small kindnesses.
                    —FREDERICK W. ROBERTSON

❀ ❀

I say it's a darn good day
when a man can put on his shoes
and go to work.
                    —JOHN BURNES

We begin to walk
on the road to happiness
when we learn the art
of relaxation.
When we learn
that relaxation is a habit
we can all acquire,
a healthy habit every day,
like brushing our teeth.

—MAXWELL MALTZ

In the pursuit of happiness
half the world is on the wrong scent.
They think it consists
in having and getting,
and in being served by others.
Happiness is really found in giving
and in serving others.

—HENRY DRUMMOND

He who can no longer
pause to wonder
and stand rapt in awe
is as good as dead.

—ALBERT EINSTEIN

❀ ❀

Happiness
is helping others!

The world is full of wonders and miracles
but man takes his little hand
and covers his eyes
and sees nothing.

—ISRAEL BAAL SHEM

Love

The language that God hears best
is the silent language of love.
       —SAINT JOHN OF THE CROSS

❀   ❀

Do not be afraid of showing affection.
Be warm and tender,
thoughtful and affectionate.
Men are more helped by sympathy
than by service.
Love is more than money,
and a kind word
will give more pleasure than a present.
       —JOHN LUBBOCK

Whoever has
a heart full of love
always has
something to give.
—POPE JOHN XXIII

❀ ❀

If a thought comes to you
of doing a kindness to some one
do it that very minute!
Don't put it off; don't wait!
What's the use of doing a kindness
if you do it a day too late?

The most important thing a father
can do for his children
is to love their mother.
          —THEODORE HESBURGH

❀ ❀

Every year that I live
I am more convinced
that the waste of life lies
in the love we have not given,
the powers we have not used,
the selfish prudence which will risk nothing,
and which, shirking pain,
misses happiness as well.

If you are suffering
from a bad man's injustice,
forgive him,
lest there be two bad men.

Life is made up,
not of great sacrifices and duties,
but of little things,
in which smiles and kindnesses,
and small obligations,
given habitually,
are what win and preserve the heart
and secure comfort.

—SIR HUMPHRY DAVY

There is nothing which cannot be borne
with cheerful alacrity
by those who love one another.
—SAINT THERESA

A loving heart is the truest wisdom.
—CHARLES DICKENS

Whether a man really loves God
can be determined
by the love he bears his fellow men.
—LEVI YITZHOK

I shall not pass
this way again.
Any good thing that I can do,
or any kindness
that I can show,
let me do it *now!*
Let me not defer it
or neglect it.
For I shall not pass
this way again.

❀ ❀

Where there is no love,
put love
and you will find love.

—SAINT JOHN OF THE CROSS

If you truly love God,
you will love your neighbor.
It does not make any difference
if he loves you or not.

—FATHER THOMAS AUGUSTINE
JUDGE, M.S.SS.T.

The best portion of
a good man's life
is his little nameless,
unremembered acts
of kindness and of love.

—WILLIAM WORDSWORTH

Love blinds us to faults,
hatred to virtues.

—MOSES IBN EZRA

He who loves
brings God and the world
together.

—MARTIN BUBER

Love is the master key
that opens the gates of happiness

The more one loves
the nearer he approaches God,
for God is the spirit
of infinite love.

—R. W. TRINE

We must be patient
with our friends
as we must be forgiving
to our enemies.

—FATHER THOMAS AUGUSTINE
JUDGE, M.S.SS.T.

Love a man even in his sin,
for that is the semblance of Divine Love,
and is the highest love on earth.

While faith makes all things possible,
it is love
that makes all things easy.

—EVAN H. HOPKINS

❁ ❁ ❁

Beauty

In every man's heart
there is a secret nerve
that answers to the vibrations of beauty.
— CHRISTOPHER MORLEY

❁ ❁

Never lose an opportunity
of seeing anything that is beautiful;
for beauty is God's handwriting—
a wayside sacrament.
Welcome it in every fair face,
in every fair sky,
in every fair flower,
and thank God for it
as a cup of blessing.
— RALPH WALDO EMERSON

Beauty raises our spirits,
temporarily takes us out of ourselves,
and makes us feel closer to God.
        —EDITH WILKINSON

In all ranks of life
the human heart yearns for the beautiful;
and the beautiful things that God makes
are His gift to all alike.
        —HARRIET BEECHER STOWE

Love of beauty
and of all lovely and wonderful things
is indispensable for our growth.
It brings reverence
and a sense of transcendence
into personal love,
and indeed into all of life.
In the words of a poet, who was also
a man of science, Robert Bridges:
"Love is a fire in whose devouring flames
all earthly ills are consumed."

—JULIAN HUXLEY

The longer I live
the more beautiful life becomes.
The earth's beauty grows on man.
If you foolishly ignore beauty,
you'll find yourself without it.
Your life will be impoverished.
But if you wisely invest in beauty,
it will remain with you
all the days of your life.
　　　　　　—FRANK LLOYD WRIGHT

Every April
God rewrites the book of Genesis.
　　　　　—AUSTIN O'MALLEY

Next to beauty
is the power of appreciating it.
—MARGARET FULLER

❀ ❀

How much is a sunset worth?
There are such things
as a sunset or a beautiful sunrise
that have no price.
Their value
is what they do for you
or to you.
Each one of us has only
so many sunsets and sunrises.
Let us learn to enjoy them
each day to the fullest.

Why should we think
about things that are lovely?
Because thinking determines life.
It is a common mistake
to blame life upon environment.
Environment modifies
but does not govern life.
The soul is stronger
than its surroundings.

—WILLIAM JAMES

A greater poverty
than that caused by lack of money
is the poverty of unawareness.
Men and women go about the world
unaware of the beauty,
the goodness, and the glories in it.
Their souls are poor.
It is better to have a poor pocketbook
than to suffer from a poor soul.

       —JERRY FLEISHMAN

The universe is to be valued
because there is truth and beauty in it;
and we live to discover
the truth and beauty
no less than to do what is right.
Indeed, we cannot attain
to that state of mind
in which we naturally do what is right
unless we are aware
of the truth and the beauty of the universe.

—A. CLUTTON-BROCK

❀ ❀ ❀

Serenity

Do not be anxious
about tomorrow
for tomorrow
will have anxieties
of its own.
Sufficient for the day
is its own trouble.

—MATT. 6:34

❀   ❀

O God, give us the courage
to accept with serenity
the things we cannot change.
Give us the courage to change
the things that should be changed.
And give us the wisdom to distinguish
the one from the other.

—REINHOLD NIEBUHR

The fullness of life does not come
from the things outside us.
We ourselves must create the beauty
in which we live.

—C. E. COWMAN

❀ ❀

A time of quietude
brings things into proportion
and gives us strength.
We all need to take time
from the busyness of living,
even if it be only ten minutes
to watch the sun go down
or the city lights
blossom against a canyoned sky.
We need time to dream,
time to remember,
and time to reach toward the infinite.
Time to be.

—GLADYS TABER

Anyone can carry his burden
however heavy,
till nightfall.
Anyone can do his work,
however hard,
for one day.
Anyone can live sweetly,
patiently, lovingly, purely,
till the sun goes down.
And this is all that life
ever really means.

—CHARLES B. NEWCOMB

❀   ❀

Patience is the key to content.

Enjoy your life
without comparing it
with that of others.
                    —CONDORCET

❁   ❁

The serene silent beauty
of a holy life
is the most powerful influence in the world,
next to the might of God.

❁   ❁

Learn the fine art of forgetting.
Do not bring the troubles of yesterday
into today.
Do not cry over spilt milk.

The safest place in all this world
is the place of duty.
God's wings are over it
and God's peace guards it.

Do not wish to be anything
but what you are,
and try to be that perfectly.

—SAINT FRANCIS DE SALES

Contentment,
and indeed usefulness,
comes as the infallible result
of great acceptances,
great humilities.

It is not so much a question
of our being set
at this or that employment,
as the spirit in which we do the work
God gives us to hand.
>   —FATHER THOMAS AUGUSTINE
>   JUDGE, M.S.SS.T.

Calmness is the rarest quality
in human life.
It is the poise of a great nature,
in harmony with life
and its ideals.
>   —WILLIAM G. JORDAN

The load of tomorrow,
added to that of yesterday,
carried today, makes the strongest falter.
We must learn to shut out the future
as tightly as the past.
                    —SIR WILLIAM OSLER

A sunny disposition
is the very soul of success.
It enables a man
to do double the labor
that he could without it,
and to do it
with half the physical and mental exhaustion.
                    —WILLIAM MATTHEWS

Be happy and considerate.
It's the one thing you can do
even if you are broke.
Courtesy is contagious.
—R. W. DALE

Have courage for the great sorrows of life
and patience for the small ones.
And when you have finished
your daily task,
go to sleep in peace.
God is awake.
—VICTOR HUGO

We cannot control the tragic
things that happen to us, but
we can control the way we
face up to them.

❀ ❀

Sooner or later, a man,
if he is wise,
discovers that life is a mixture
of good days and bad,
victory and defeat,
give and take.

—WILFERD PETERSON

Slow me down, Lord.
Slow me down!

Ease the pounding of my heart
by the quieting of my mind.

Steady my hurried pace
with a vision of the eternal reach of time.

Give me, amid the confusion of the day,
the calmness of the everlasting hills.

Break the tension of my nerves and muscles
with the soothing music
of the singing streams that live in my memory.
Help me to know the magical,
restoring power of sleep.

Teach me the art of taking minute vacations.
Of slowing down to look at a flower,
to chat with a friend, to pat a dog,
to read a few lines from a good book.

Remind me each day
of the fable of the hare and the tortoise,
that I may know that the race
is not always to the swift—
that there is more to life
than increasing its speed.

Let me look upward
into the branches of the flowering oak
and know that it grew great and strong
because it grew slowly and well.

Slow me down, Lord,
and inspire me to send my roots
deep into the soil of life's enduring values
that I may grow toward the stars
of my greater destiny.

     —WILFERD PETERSON

You are never fully dressed
until you wear a smile.

The important thing
is to know how to take
all things quietly.
                —MICHAEL FARADAY

❀ ❀ ❀

Faith

How much is lost
to those who have no faith!
To them human existence
is an enigma
and man's wanderings on this planet
are a delirium.
—FATHER THOMAS AUGUSTINE
JUDGE, M.S.SS.T.

❀ ❀

Nothing in life is more wonderful than faith—
the one great moving force
we can neither weigh in the balance
nor test in the crucible!
—SIR WILLIAM OSLER

Life, if we are to be victors over it,
not victims of it,
is an adventure in faith.
Faith in God,
faith in the immortal soul within us,
faith in life and in our fellow men.
Without faith, the plus quality,
we cannot really live.

     —JOSEPH F. NEWTON

Somehow, I am necessary for God's purpose,
as necessary in my place
as an archangel in his.

     —CARDINAL NEWMAN

During the past thirty years,
people from all civilized countries
on the earth have consulted me.
Among all my patients
in the second half of life—
that is to say, over thirty-five—
there has not been one whose problem
in the last resort
was not that of finding
a religious outlook on life.
It is safe to say that every one of them
fell ill
because he had lost
that which the living religions
of every age
have given their followers,
and none of them has been really healed
who did not regain his religious outlook.

—DR. C. G. JUNG

Every tomorrow has two handles
We can take hold of it
by the handle of anxiety
or the handle of faith.

Let your belief in God be seen.
Lamps do not talk, but they do shine.
A lighthouse sounds no drum,
it beats no gong;
yet, far over the waters,
its friendly light
is seen by the mariner.

—THEODORE L. CUYLER

Religion is the first thing
and the last thing,
and until a man has found God
he begins at no beginning,
he works to no end.

Religion is the light of our lives.
Faith is the key
that turns it on.

—ERNIE FORD

The most beautiful thing man can do
is to forgive.

—ELEAZAR BEN JUDAH

If I can put
one touch of rosy sunset
into the life
of any man or woman,
I shall feel that I
have worked with God.

The practice of religion
is indispensable for peace of mind
because it blesses us
with inner gifts
beyond the bestowal of any science;
a sense of our purpose in the world,
a feeling of relatedness to God.

—JOSHUA LOTH LIEBMAN

Real security
is having a sense of God.
To know God
is to be adjusted
to everyday living.

—A. A. M.

When I accept the will of God
with regard to myself,
my life, and every detail of my life,
just as it comes,
with all its limitations and frustrations,
I am entering into communion
with God.

—CARDINAL SUENENS

Do not look forward
to what might happen tomorrow!
The same Everlasting Father
who cares for you today
will take care of you tomorrow.
Either He will shield you
from suffering,
or He will give you unfailing strength
to bear it.
Be at peace then
and put aside all anxious thoughts
and imaginations.

—SAINT FRANCIS DE SALES

Faith is one of the forces
by which men live,
and the total absence of it
means collapse.

—WILLIAM JAMES

Sometimes we think of religion
as taking all the joy out of life,
but, instead,
it is like finding buried treasure,
like finding a perfect jewel.

—CHARLES ALLEN

Above all am I convinced of the need,
irrevocable and inescapable,
of every human heart for God.
No matter how we try to escape,
to lose ourselves in restless seeking,
we cannot separate ourselves
from our divine source.
There is no substitute for God.

—A. J. CRONIN

Only God can fully satisfy
the hungry heart of man.
—HUGH BLACK

In nothing do men come closer to God
than in doing good
to their fellow man.

Science can tell us how
to do more and more things;
it cannot tell us
what ought to be done.
—JOSEPH WOOD KRUTCH

You are made for God,
just as your eye is made for light.
You cannot see in the dark.
You cannot find peace
except in the will of God,
for "In His will is our peace."

❁ ❁

Vital religious faith
is the most important single thing
in a man's personal health.
—KRISTOFER HAGEN

Faith draws the poison from every grief,
takes the sting from every loss,
and quenches the fire of every pain;
and only faith can do it.
                    —J. G. HOLLAND

❀ ❀

We know not what the future holds,
but we do know
who holds the future.

❀ ❀ ❀

Prayer

The greatest thing the greatest man
ever did was pray.
                    —A. W. HARE

❁   ❁

Prayer is not only worship;
it is also an invisible emanation
of man's worshiping spirit—
the most powerful form of energy
that one can generate.
                    —ALEXIS CARREL

Change can be accomplished
most of all through prayer,
because with God
all things are possible.
                    —WILFERD PETERSON

❀ ❀

There is not in the world
a kind of life
more sweet and delightful
than that of a continual conversation
with God.
                    —BROTHER LAWRENCE

If you are too busy to pray,
you are too busy.

The haste of modern living
is waste in the truest, deepest sense.
We are so busy
reaching for things beyond us
that we miss the eternal values
which are near at hand.
In our hurry and fret
we have forgotten
how to walk and talk with God.

Prayer is a force as real
as terrestrial gravity.
As a physician, I have seen men,
after all therapy had failed,
lifted out of disease and melancholy
by the serene effort of prayer.
Only in prayer do we achieve
that complete and harmonious assembly
of body, mind and spirit
which gives the frail human need
its unshakable strength.

—ALEXIS CARREL

More things are wrought by prayer
Than this world dreams of.
       —ALFRED, LORD TENNYSON

The will of God
is learned in prayer.
There we become courageous.

Dear God be good to me.
Your sea is so wide,
and my boat is so small!

Be not forgetful of prayer.
Everytime you pray
there will be new feeling
and new meaning in it,
which will give you fresh courage.
—LEO TOLSTOY

Most of us wait until we're in trouble,
and then we pray like the dickens.
Wonder what would happen if,
some morning, we'd wake up and say,
"Anything I can do for *You* today, Lord?"
—BURTON HILLIS

I know not by what methods rare,
But this I know—God answers prayer.
I know not when He sends the word
That tells us fervent prayer is heard.
I know it cometh—soon or late;
Therefore we need to pray and wait.
I know not if the blessing sought
Will come in just the way I thought
I leave my prayers with Him alone,
Whose Will is wiser than my own!

❀ ❀ ❀

The
Understanding
Heart

No one knows another man's burden.

❁ ❁

The art of being wise
is the art
of knowing what to overlook.
— WILLIAM JAMES

❁ ❁

A man's true wealth
is the good he does
in this world.

How few our real wants,
and how vast our imaginary ones!
　　　　—JOHANN KASPAR LAVATER

Great Spirit,
help me never to judge another
until I have walked in his moccasins
for two weeks.
　　　　—SIOUX INDIAN PRAYER

If we want to master fear and worry
we must not only be willing
to accept help from others,
but also learn
to accept ourselves,
with our limitations
as well as our abilities.

—JOSHUA LOTH LIEBMAN

The primary thing is
not to tell everyone his duty,
but to do one's own.

—VINCENT MCNABB, O.P.

The greatest mistake
you can make in life
is to be continually fearing
that you will make one.

—ELBERT HUBBARD

Besides the noble art of getting things done,
there is the noble art
of leaving things undone.
The wisdom of life
consists in the elimination of nonessentials.

—LIN YUTANG

The essence of evil
is to think of oneself and of other people
simply as perishable by-products
of an impersonal nature,
and to live accordingly.
The essence of good
is to think of oneself and others
as children of God,
and to live accordingly.

❀ ❀

To err is human;
to forgive divine.
                    —ALEXANDER POPE

I want not only to be loved,
but to be told that I am loved.
The realm of silence
is large enough beyond the grave.
—GEORGE ELIOT

A smile of encouragement at the right moment
can act like sunlight
on a closed-up flower.
It may be the turning point
for a struggling life.

Teach me, Lord,
to be patient,
and help me to use
every minute in Thy service,
that of Thy gifts
nothing may be lost or wasted.

❁ ❁

If a man does not keep pace
with his companions,
perhaps it is because he hears
a different drummer.
Let him step to the music he hears,
however measured or far away.

—HENRY DAVID THOREAU

You will find,
as you look back upon your life,
that the moments that stand out
are the moments
when you have done things
for others.
—HENRY DRUMMOND

If I can stop one heart from breaking,
I shall not live in vain;
If I can ease one life the aching,
Or cool one pain
Or help one fainting robin
Unto his nest again
I shall not live in vain.
—EMILY DICKINSON

I complained because I had no shoes,
until I met a man who had no feet!
—SPANISH PROVERB

Life is short
and we have not too much time
for gladdening the hearts
of those who are traveling
the dark way with us.
Oh, be swift to love!
Make haste to be kind!
—HENRI F. AMIEL

In this life,
if you have anything to pardon,
pardon quickly.
Slow forgiveness
is little better than no forgiveness.

—SIR ARTHUR WING PINERO

Do not keep the elaborate boxes
of your love and tenderness
sealed up until your friends are dead.
Fill their lives with sweetness.
Speak approving, cheering words
while their ears can hear them
and their hearts be thrilled by them.

—HENRY WARD BEECHER

❀ ❀ ❀

Growing
Old

Grow old along with me!
The best is yet to be.
The last of life, for which the first was made:
Our times are in His hand
Who saith, "A whole I planned.
Youth shows but half; trust God;
see all, nor be afraid!"
                    —ROBERT BROWNING

If wrinkles must be written upon our house,
let them not be written upon the heart.
The spirit should not grow old.
                    —JAMES A. GARFIELD

Growing old, let me grow lovely.
Laces, and ivory, and gold,
And silks need not be new.
And there is healing in old trees;
Old streets a glamour hold.
Why may not I, as well as these,
Grow lovely, growing old?
—KARLE WILSON BAKER

Whatever a man's age,
he can reduce it several years
by putting a bright-colored flower
in his buttonhole.
—MARK TWAIN

I like spring, but it is too young.
I like summer, but it is too proud.
So I like best of all autumn;
because its leaves are a little yellow,
its tone mellower,
its colors richer.
And it is tinged a little with sorrow.
Its golden richness speaks
not of the innocence of spring,
nor of the power of summer,
but of the mellowness and kindly wisdom
of approaching age.
It knows the limitations of life
and is content.

—LIN YUTANG

For I reckon that the sufferings
of this present time
are not worthy to be compared
with the glory
which shall be revealed in us.

—ROM. 8:18

A man's age is as unimportant
as the size of his shoes
if his interest in life is not impaired,
if he is compassionate,
and if time has mellowed
his prejudices.

To be seventy years young
is sometimes
far more cheerful and hopeful
than to be
forty years old.

    —OLIVER WENDELL HOLMES

We are on our way home
and the trials and thorns
must be gently brushed aside
so as not to interrupt us
on our way.

    —MOTHER CORNELIA CONNELLY

To know how to grow old
is the masterwork of wisdom,
and one of the most difficult chapters
in the great art of living.
—HENRI F. AMIEL

As for old age, embrace and love it.
It abounds with pleasure
if you know how to use it.
The gradually declining years
are among the sweetest in a man's life;
and I maintain that even when
they have reached the extreme limit,
they have their pleasures still.
—SENECA

I shall grow old,
but never lose life's zest,
because the road's last turn
will be the best.
　　　—HENRY VAN DYKE

❀　❀

Given three requisites—
means of existence,
reasonable health,
and an absorbing interest—
the years beyond sixty
can be the happiest and most satisfying
of a lifetime.
　　　—EARNEST ELMO CALKINS

Some lives, like evening primroses,
blossom most beautifully
in the evening of life.
  —C. E. COWMAN

Death is not extinguishing the light;
it is putting out the lamp
because the dawn has come.
  —PAUL S. MCELROY

O Lord,
support us all the day long
of this troublous life,
until the shades lengthen
and the evening comes,
and the busy world is hushed,
the fever of life is over,
and our work is done.

Then, Lord, in Thy mercy
grant us safe lodging,
a holy rest,
and peace at the last,
through Jesus Christ our Lord. Amen.
—CARDINAL NEWMAN

It is magnificent to grow old,
if one keeps young.
—HARRY EMERSON FOSDICK

❀ ❀

Many blessings do the advancing years
bring with them.
—HORACE

❀ ❀

Winter is on my head,
but spring is in my heart.
—VICTOR HUGO

To me, old age is always
fifteen years older than I am.
—BERNARD BARUCH

About the Author

The Very Reverend Gilbert Hay, M.S.SS.T., was born in Kearny, New Jersey, and is the third member of his immediate family to enter the religious life. He was ordained in 1940 and subsequently served for ten years with the Missionary Servants of the Most Holy Trinity in Alabama and Mississippi, where he founded St. Peter Trinity Mission at Holy Trinity, Alabama, and Holy Child Jesus Mission, Canton, Mississippi. Since 1951 Father Gilbert has been Mission Procurator for Trinity Missions, with the responsibility of providing for ninety-three missions in fourteen states and Puerto Rico.

In 1966 the Catholic University of America named Father Gilbert Missionary of the Year.